P9-BYE-400

IN THEIR OWN WORDS

HARRIET TUBMAN

George Sullivan

LIBRARY OF CONGRESS CATALOGING-IN-PUBLICATION DATA

Sullivan, George, 1927–
Harriet Tubman/George Sullivan
p.   cm.—(In their own words)
Includes bibliographical references (p.) and index.
Summary: Using a variety of primary sources, this biography of Harriet Tubman describes
the life of a former slave who was responsible for helping many other slaves to freedom.
1. Tubman, Harriet, 1820?–1913—Juvenile literature.   2. Slaves—United States—
Biography—Juvenile literature.   3. Afro-American women—Biography—Juvenile
literature.   4. Afro-Americans—Biography—Juvenile literature.   5. Underground
railroad—Juvenile literature.   [1. Tubman, Harriet, 1820?–1913.   2. Slaves.
3. Afro-Americans—Biography.   4. Women—Biography.   5. Underground railroad.]
I. Title.   II. In their own words (Scholastic)
E444.T82 S85   2001
305.5′67′092—dc21   00-030065
[B]   CIP

ISBN 0-439-16584-9

10 9 8 7 6 5 4 3 2 1   01 02 03 04 05

Composition by Brad Walrod
Printed in the U.S.A.   40
First printing, January 2001

CONTENTS

CHAPTER 1

INTRODUCTION

"I HAVE REASONED THIS OUT IN MY MIND. There was one of two things I had a right to, liberty or death. If I could not have one, I would have the other, for no man should take me alive. I should fight for my liberty as long as my strength lasted, and when the time came for me to go, the Lord would let them take me."

With these words, Harriet Tubman, born into slavery, prepared to make her escape to freedom in the North. She risked capture, a brutal beating, and even death.

Harriet Tubman's words show her to be bold and brave and a person of great faith. She died almost a century ago, but her words still inspire Americans today.

Harriet Tubman did make her escape. But afterward, she did not feel completely happy. She felt great sorrow for those who remained in bondage. So she returned to the South again and again on rescue missions. She guided more slaves to freedom on the Underground Railroad than any other person.

In seeking to learn about Harriet Tubman, or any other person from the historic past, students rely on both primary and secondary sources.

Primary sources are actual records that have been handed down from the past. They can take many different forms. Lincoln's Gettysburg Address is a primary source. Tax records and census records are primary sources. So are diaries, maps, postcards, and movie ticket stubs.

A secondary source is the description of an event written by someone who did not witness it. Encyclopedias are secondary sources. A history textbook is a secondary source.

Primary sources that relate to Harriet Tubman are very rare. Official records were seldom kept to

Harriet Tubman, the remarkable woman who was born a slave and died a hero

document the lives of slaves. No birth certificate was issued when Harriet Tubman was born. There are no grade school or high school records for her. Harriet Tubman never had a day of school.

In 1869, when Harriet was approaching her fiftieth birthday, her life story was published. *Scenes in the Life of Harriet Tubman* is the book's title. It was written by Sarah Bradford, a Geneva, New York, schoolteacher and close friend of Harriet's. Much of the information in the book is based on her conversations with Harriet. In 1886, Bradford wrote a second book about Harriet called *Harriet: The Moses of Her People*.

These books have some of the features of a primary source. They contain many passages in Harriet's own words. These quotations are valuable. They help us understand Harriet's thoughts and feelings.

Before the Civil War, Harriet Tubman worked hard to help people who wanted to end slavery. They were called abolitionists. In letters, books, and articles, the leading abolitionists of the time often hailed her work.

These documents are primary sources, too. They show how Harriet Tubman was thought of by people of her day.

This book tells the story of this remarkable woman. Throughout her long and often difficult life, she served as a symbol of strength and courage for her people.

NOT WORTH A SIXPENCE

"I GREW UP LIKE A WEED—IGNORANT OF liberty, having no experience of it," Harriet Tubman once said of her childhood in slavery. "I was not happy or contented. Every time I saw a white man I was afraid of being carried away. We were always uneasy."

Harriet Tubman was born in 1820 or 1821 in Bucktown, Maryland. She was the youngest of eleven children.

Harriet was never certain about her birth date, and for good reason. Slave masters seldom kept written accounts of the births and deaths of the people they owned. The slaves themselves, unable to read or write, kept no records either.

Bucktown was a small and quiet settlement of no more than a dozen houses. It had a store, a church, and a post office.

From the town's crossroads, flat black farmland stretched in every direction. Beyond the farms were woodlands and swamps.

Harriet and her family were the property of Edward Brodess, who owned a farm on the Big Buckwater River. Brodess harvested corn, wheat, and rye. His woodlands were rich in tall oak and loblolly pine. He sold timber to shipbuilders.

Brodess also earned money from his slaves. Many were hired out to other farmers in the area. Brodess was paid for the work his slaves did for the farmers.

In times of financial need, Brodess sometimes sold his slaves. As a result, wives could be taken from their husbands. Children could be separated from their parents. Harriet and her family lived in constant fear of having their family ripped apart.

At the time of Harriet Tubman's birth, there were about two million men, women, and children in the

This metal highway sign marks Harriet Tubman's Bucktown, Maryland, birthplace.

United States who were slaves. A high percentage of these came from West Africa.

That is where Harriet Tubman's ancestors had lived. Harriet sometimes recalled that she was "one of those Ashantis." Powerful warriors, the Ashanti conquered many of their West African neighbors.

Harriet's grandparents on both sides had been brought from West Africa in chains. Their children were automatically born into lives of slavery.

When Harriet was born, her name was derived from the names of her parents. From her mother, Harriet Greene, she inherited the name Harriet. From her father, Benjamin Ross, she got her last name. She was called Harriet Ross.

Harriet's father, "Old Ben," as he was called, spent his days cutting timber for Brodess. Her mother, known as "Rit," worked as a servant in the Brodess family home. To the slaves, it was known as "the big house."

A few weeks after Harriet was born, her mother had to return to work for the Brodess family. Harriet and other slave infants and small children were looked after by older slave women.

Like the other children, Harriet wore what looked like a sack made of coarse cloth, with holes for her arms and neck. The children always went barefoot.

Young slave children at play. Their master's house is on the left; slave cabins are on the right.

When Harriet was about six, she became a source of profit to Brodess. She was hired out to a couple named Cook. Harriet was terrified at the thought of leaving her home and family. But she had no choice.

Life was harsh for Harriet at the Cook home. At night, she was made to sleep on the kitchen floor. Her meals were table scraps.

Mrs. Cook was a weaver, turning plantation cotton into cloth the family needed. She tried to teach Harriet how to weave. But Harriet would not learn. She hated Mrs. Cook. She wanted to go home.

Mr. Cook was a trapper. When Harriet failed her weaving lessons, he put her to work watching his muskrat traps.

Mr. Cook set the traps along the banks of a river that flowed past the house. Harriet's job was to wade along the river's edge, looking for trapped muskrats.

Harriet liked being outdoors. She didn't seem to mind the hard work. Then winter approached. The river turned icy cold. Harriet had no boots for her feet. She had no jacket or coat to keep herself warm. Yet she was sent out each morning to check the trap lines.

Soon Harriet was sneezing and coughing. Before long, she developed a high fever. Then one morning,

Bucktown, Maryland, is known for its flat black farmland and dense forests.

she awoke to find her body covered with red spots. Besides a bad cough, Harriet had a case of the measles.

The Cooks did not wish to care for a sick black child. They took Harriet back to the Brodess plantation. There her mother nursed her back to health.

As soon as Harriet was well, Brodess hired her

out again. She was put in a wagon and dropped off at the home of a woman known to Harriet as Miss Susan. Miss Susan was seeking a baby nurse and a housekeeper. Harriet was expected to do both jobs.

Harriet was the child's nurse at night. She did housework during the day.

Each night, after her day of household work, Harriet was made to care for the baby while everyone else slept. She had to rock the baby's cradle so the child wouldn't cry. But sometimes Harriet would fall asleep. The cradle would stop rocking. The baby would awaken and begin to cry, waking the mother.

Miss Susan would leap out of bed. She instantly grabbed a whip and would start beating Harriet.

Many years later, Harriet's biographer, Sarah Bradford, would write, "[Harriet's] poor neck is even now covered with scars...."

Harriet became weak from the beatings. She was exhausted from not being able to sleep at night.

Miss Susan had no more use for Harriet. She sent her back to Brodess. "That girl isn't worth a sixpence," she told him.

Harriet's mother nursed her daughter back to health. But both knew that once Harriet had regained her strength, Brodess would try to hire her out again.

BRUSH WITH DEATH

L ATE IN THE SUMMER OF 1831, WHEN Harriet was about eleven, the slaves on the Brodess farm heard startling news. In nearby Southampton County, Virginia, a slave and preacher named Nat Turner led a slave revolt. The uprising was quickly crushed. But Turner and his followers killed some sixty whites. The victims included Turner's owner.

Although Turner went into hiding, he was soon captured. He and thirty other blacks were hanged.

White slave owners became fearful after the revolt. Many Southern states passed laws to tighten the controls on slaves. Slaves could no

Nat Turner was captured, tried, and hanged, but his revolt struck terror into the hearts of Southern slave owners.

longer travel as easily from one place to another. It became illegal to teach a slave to read or write.

But Nat Turner became a hero to the slaves. His revolt sparked the hope of freedom in their hearts.

Harriet had a good idea of what it meant to be free. While Dorchester County was populated by several thousand slaves, it was also home to many free blacks. Some former slaves had been able to buy their freedom. Others had been born of free parents.

Many slaves sought their freedom by the simple act of running away. Some reached the North and freedom. But others were caught and brought back. Often they tried escaping again. A North Carolina woman was known to have run away from her plantation no less than sixteen times.

Sometimes Harriet would be awakened at night by shouts of angry men and then furious hoofbeats. She knew that a slave had run away. The men on horseback, called patrollers, were hunting him down.

Harriet herself became caught up in one slave's attempt to escape. Her involvement ended in disaster.

At the time, Harriet was working as a field hand. Edward Brodess had realized that Harriet was never going to become a household worker. He began to hire her out as a farm laborer instead.

Harriet worked in the cornfields. She plowed,

planted, and hoed. She loaded heavy vegetables into wagons. She drove oxen in the field.

It was backbreaking work for the young teenager. But in time, Harriet got used to it. Her muscles hardened. She got so good at it that she could astonish men with her strength.

One day in the fall of 1835, Harriet was shucking corn with slaves from her own and other plantations. She looked up to see a tall slave acting strangely. He was sneaking around, trying to hide from the overseer. Suddenly, the tall black man began to run.

The overseer saw him. He grabbed his whip and ran after him.

Without thinking, Harriet threw aside the ear of corn she was shucking. She ran after the overseer.

The tall slave kept running until he came to a crossroads. There he ran inside a small store.

The overseer ran into the store, too. He spotted the slave under a counter where he was trying to hide.

Harriet watched from the doorway as the overseer

Thousands of slaves escaped their lives of hardship by running away. This engraving pictures one fugitive who gained freedom in the North.

dragged the slave out from under the counter. He held up his whip and told the slave to prepare for a beating.

Then the overseer saw Harriet in the doorway. He told her to hold the slave while he tied him up for the lashing.

Harriet refused. She did not want to see the slave punished. Suddenly, the slave broke free of the overseer's grasp. He charged past Harriet out the door. The overseer started after him. But Harriet stood in the doorway blocking the overseer's path. The overseer grabbed a heavy lead weight from the counter and threw it at the fleeing slave.

The weight never reached its target. Instead, it struck Harriet squarely in the forehead. She dropped to the ground instantly. Blood poured from a deep wound in her forehead. She lay unconscious while the overseer ran off in pursuit of the slave.

Harriet was carried back to her parents' cabin. She remained in a coma for days. Her mother wept over her still body. She did not know whether her daughter was going to live or die.

From time to time, Brodess appeared at the cabin door and looked in on Harriet. He was angry with her for defying the overseer.

Little by little, Harriet began to recover. The wound in her head healed. But it left a deep scar.

The blow she had received caused her to suffer sudden sleeping spells. One minute Harriet would be lively and alert. Then suddenly, without warning, she would fall into a deep sleep. No one could wake her. These blackouts continued for the rest of her life.

HIRED OUT

A YEAR OR TWO AFTER HARRIET HAD been injured, Edward Brodess became ill and died. For Brodess's slaves, a time of great worry followed. Would they be sold to new owners? Would families be scattered far and wide?

Harriet had already seen a brother and a sister "sold South." They had been marched away in a chain gang. They would end up as plantation field hands. In the Deep South, slaves were forced to work harder and longer than they were in Maryland. Brutal beatings were common.

Then it became known that Brodess's will declared that none of his slaves were to be sold outside the state of Maryland. This news cheered some of the slaves. But it did not satisfy Harriet. They were still slaves. They were not free.

The will also stated that the Brodess farm would be managed by Dr. Anthony Thompson. A small, bald-headed minister in Bucktown, he was known as Doc Thompson.

Doc Thompson resumed the practice of hiring out the farm's slaves. Harriet's head wound had healed. But she still suffered severe headaches and blackouts. Nevertheless, Doc Thompson hired her out to John Stewart, a local builder. She was put to work as a maid in the Stewart home.

Harriet hated housework. She wanted to be outdoors, working in the fields or forests. Working in the Stewart home brought back memories of Miss Susan and the beatings Harriet had suffered at her hands.

Years later, Harriet recalled this period in her life. "They [the slaveholders] don't know any better; it's the way they were brought up. 'Make the little slaves mind you or flog them,' was what they said to their children, and they were brought up with the

Before the Civil War, slaves were sometimes bought and sold at the Dorchester County courthouse in Cambridge, Maryland, near Bucktown.

whip in their hands. Now that wasn't the way on all plantations; there were good masters and mistresses, as I've heard tell, but I didn't happen to come across any of them."

After months of making beds and washing clothes, Harriet couldn't stand it any longer. She went to Stewart and asked if she could work in the fields. Stewart agreed. He knew that Harriet was strong. He knew that she could do the work of a man. And, of course, she was worth more as a field hand than as a maid.

Meanwhile, Harriet's father had been put in charge of a group of slaves who cut lumber. Harriet became a member of his crew.

Harriet worked side by side with her father, Ben. She cut down trees, trimmed off the branches, and split logs.

Stewart was impressed with the way Harriet worked. He was so pleased that he allowed her to "hire her time." When she had finished her work, she could take extra jobs from other people and charge them for her services. She had to give Stewart part of the money that she earned, however.

Harriet had little trouble finding additional work. She drove oxen and plowed the cornfields on neighboring farms. She chopped and hauled wood. She was able to save a small amount of money for herself.

By now, Harriet was about five feet tall, as tall as she would ever be. She was lean and very strong. She had a large mouth and a rocklike chin. She always wore a colorful bandanna about her head.

Harriet loved working with her father and being outdoors from daybreak until dusk.

CASH!

All persons that have SLAVES to dispose of, will do well by giving me a call, as I will give the

HIGHEST PRICE FOR

Men, Women, &

CHILDREN.

Any person that wishes to sell, will call at Hill's tavern, or at Shannon Hill for me, and any information they want will be promptly attended to.

Thomas Griggs.

Charlestown, May 7, 1835.

PRINTED AT THE FREE PRESS OFFICE, CHARLESTOWN.

This handbill dating to the 1830s documents a busy market for slaves— "Men, Women, & Children."

But there were days she was made to feel like a slave, like a piece of property. Sometimes Stewart would bring guests to the farm. He would entertain them by having Harriet show off her strength, which was equal to that of most men. Stewart would order a boat to be filled with stones. Harriet would be hitched to the boat like an ox or a mule. Pulling from the riverbank, Harriet would be made to haul the very heavy boat upstream. Stewart's friends would ooh and aah at Harriet's strength.

Harriet felt saddened and humiliated by these displays. In some ways, they were worse than the beatings she had received at the hands of Miss Susan.

During the many weeks that Harriet had been recovering from her head injury, she kept having a dream. In it the words, "Arise, flee for your life," were repeated to her.

And in the dream, she saw horsemen coming. She heard the shrieks of women and children as they were being torn from one another. Women were motioning Harriet to come toward them. She seemed to see a line that divided the land of slavery from the land of freedom. On the far side of the line were green fields and lovely flowers. Beautiful white ladies were waiting to welcome her, to care for her.

More and more, Harriet thought about crossing that line.

JOHN TUBMAN

IN 1831, A SLAVE NAMED TICE DAVIDS fled from a Kentucky plantation. Upon learning of his escape, his master went after him.

Tice Davids hurried north until he reached the Ohio River. Somehow he managed to get across. His master followed in a small boat. On the opposite shore, the master was unable to pick up Davids's trail. Tice Davids had disappeared.

The master shook his head in frustration. "He must have gone on an underground road," he said.

From that incident, the term "Underground Railroad" was born. Of course, it was neither beneath the ground nor a railroad. It was the term used to define the system by which Northerners helped runaway slaves escape to freedom.

Other railroad terms were used to describe how the system worked. A station was a safe house, a place where a runaway slave could hide.

People who provided shelter for runaways were known as railroad agents, conductors, or station masters.

All lines of the Underground Railroad led north. Some stretched through Ohio, Indiana, and Illinois. In the East, the railroad traveled through Pennsylvania, New Jersey, and New York.

As Harriet toiled in the fields and forests of Dorchester County, she heard tales of the Underground Railroad. She heard stories of whites helping blacks to escape. Whites helping blacks? To Harriet, that seemed unbelievable.

All that was happening caused turmoil in Harriet's mind. She wasn't sure what to do. Should she try to gain her freedom and risk the dangers of an attempted escape? Or should she continue her life as a slave and face its many cruelties?

This engraving of a fleeing slave sometimes appeared on wanted posters that offered rewards for the capture of runaways.

Harriet eventually decided to postpone any plans to run off. One reason was because she met and fell in love with John Tubman. He lived in a cabin near the Brodess farm.

John Tubman was black. But he was not a slave. His mother and father had been slaves. But when their master died, his will had freed his slaves. John Tubman's mother and father thereby gained their freedom. When John was born, he was born free.

John was not like most other people that Harriet knew. John could read. He could write. Sometimes he read her stories.

Harriet and John were married in 1844. She was about twenty-three years old.

Harriet's marriage did not change her status. She remained a slave. Being married meant only that she was permitted to share her husband's cabin at night.

The situation made Harriet curious about her legal status. What made John Tubman free? What made her a slave?

Harriet paid a lawyer $5 to look into her mother's records at the Dorchester County courthouse. The lawyer discovered the will of her mother's old master. The will stated that her mother was to become the property of Mary Patterson upon the master's death. Further, the will declared that Harriet's mother was to be given her freedom when she reached the age of forty-five.

But Mary Patterson died young. Harriet's mother had then been sold. The lawyer told Harriet that her mother should not have been sold, that her mother was legally free. Because her mother should have been granted her freedom, Harriet was also supposed to be free.

But there was nothing that could be done about the situation, the lawyer told her. Too much time

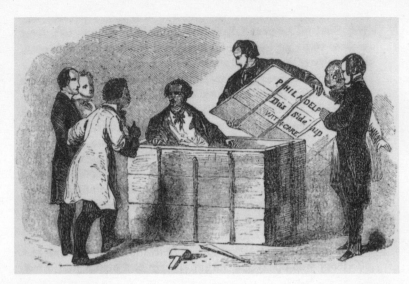

Henry Brown, a slave, paid a friend $40 to box him up and ship him to freedom in the North. Afterward, he came to be known as "Box" Brown.

had passed. No one would listen to Harriet and her claim now.

Harriet began to feel that she had been tricked into slavery. Her bitterness deepened. She kept thinking of escape and freedom.

She now knew that it was only a matter of time before she would flee.

ESCAPE

HARRIET TOLD HER HUSBAND OF
her dream of freedom. John laughed
at her. He told her she was foolish.

John Tubman had no wish to go north. He was
free and happy with his life. He had a roof over
his head. He had all the food that he wanted.
And he had Harriet, who loved him and was
happy to share with him the little money she was
earning.

Harriet's plans to flee north to freedom
disturbed John. He told her that if she tried to
escape, he would tell Doc Thompson.

Harriet knew what that meant. The news
would quickly pass to every slaveholder in the
area. Alarm bells would sound. Posters would be

hung everywhere. Mounted patrollers with their guns and bloodhounds would try to track her down. A harsh beating could result.

Harriet was shocked that her husband would think of betraying her. But it didn't change her mind. It only meant that her plans would not include him.

One day in 1849, about five years after Harriet's marriage, news swept the slave quarters that Doc Thompson planned to sell some of the slaves. He needed money. Then came news that jolted Harriet. Two of her sisters had already been sold.

Harriet now knew that she could wait no longer. She must flee now. She convinced three of her brothers to go with her.

Harriet left late that night, after John had fallen asleep. She stepped out of the cabin and dashed toward the woods. There she met her brothers.

Harriet guided her brothers through the dark woods. But they had not gone very far before her brothers became frightened. They feared they would be discovered. They urged Harriet to turn back. At

$100 REWARD!

RANAWAY

From the undersigned, living on Current River, about twelve miles above Doniphan, in Ripley County, Mo., on 2nd of March, 1860, A NEGRO MAN, about 30 years old, weighs about 160 pounds; high forehead, with a scar on it; had on brown pants and coat very much worn, and an old black wool hat; shoes size No. 11.

The above reward will be given to any person who may apprehend this said negro out of the State: and fifty dollars if apprehended in this State outside of Ripley county, or $25 if taken in Ripley county.

APOS TUCKER.

After one of Apos Tucker's slaves attempted to escape, Tucker passed out this handbill to his Ripley County, Missouri, neighbors.

first, she objected. Then Harriet realized that she was not prepared to travel by herself. She would have to turn back.

Not long after she returned, a slave from a nearby farm told Harriet that she and two of her brothers were to be sold south. They were to be carried off the very next day.

Harriet knew she must escape right away. But alone, without her brothers.

Harriet wanted to tell her family what she planned to do. She made her way to the Brodess home where her sister Mary Ann worked. There were several other slaves there. Then the master of the house rode up on horseback.

Harriet knew it would be too risky to speak to Mary Ann now. The master might get suspicious. So, in her low, deep voice, Harriet began singing. Her song was one that was often sung in church. It spoke of the Promised Land. In the Bible, it is a place of happiness.

When Mary Ann heard the song, she realized the words had a double meaning:

> *I'm sorry I'm going to leave you,*
>   *Farewell, oh farewell,*
> *But I'll meet you in the morning,*
>   *Farewell, oh farewell.*
>
> *I'll meet you in the morning,*
>   *I'm bound for the Promised Land,*
> *On the other side of the Jordan,*
>   *Bound for the Promised Land.*

That night, after John was asleep, Harriet slipped out of the cabin. She took with her a small packet of food. She also took her patchwork quilt. She had made the quilt herself, sewing together small pieces of colored cloth. It was precious to her.

Harriet headed for the home of a white woman in Bucktown who was known to help runaways. Harriet approached the home cautiously. Her heart was pounding as she tapped on the door.

The woman did not seem surprised to see Harriet. She invited her into the kitchen. They sat at the kitchen table. The woman gave Harriet the names of two people who would help her. She also gave Harriet the directions to reach the first house where she would receive food and shelter. Now Harriet was aboard the Underground Railroad.

Follow the Choptank River north to its source, the woman told her. When the river trickled to its end, Harriet should travel north and east, crossing into Delaware, which was also a slave state. Camden, Delaware, was her destination. Outside of Camden, Harriet would find a white farmhouse

Harriet Tubman is known to have been friendly with the family that owned this Bucktown home. They may have aided her in her escape.

with green shutters. That was the next station on the Underground Railroad.

Harriet was deeply grateful to the woman for her help. Before leaving, she gave the woman her prized quilt.

Harriet set out at dusk, traveling through the woods. She followed the Choptank River. She felt certain that Doc Thompson and the slave hunters would be looking for her. At daybreak, she hid herself in the underbrush and rested until sundown.

Harriet finally reached the white house with the green shutters. The mistress of the house greeted her with a smile. She then handed Harriet a broom and told her to sweep the yard.

Harriet's brow wrinkled. Why was she being put to work? Then Harriet realized that sweeping the yard was a means of disguise. No one would suspect a black woman working in a yard to be a runaway.

That night the woman's husband loaded his farm wagon with vegetables. Then he told Harriet to climb in. He covered her with blankets. Harriet listened to the clip-clop of the horses' feet as the wagon bounced along.

On the far side of Camden, at the edge of thick woods, the farmer stopped the wagon. After Harriet climbed out, he told her to continue north through the woods. He told her where she would find the next station. He also told her to travel only at night.

In the dark, Harriet followed the North Star. The

North Star can be used like a compass to travel north. Finally, thanks to those who helped her and her own faith and determination, Harriet crossed from Delaware into the free state of Pennsylvania.

Years later, she would describe how she felt. "When I had found I had crossed that line, I looked at my hands to see if I was the same person. There was such a glory over everything; the sun came like gold through the trees, and over the fields, and I felt like I was in Heaven."

FIRST PASSENGERS

H ARRIET'S GREAT JOY AT BEING free did not last very long. As she would later explain to her biographer, "I was *free*; but there was no one to welcome me to the land of freedom. I was a stranger in a strange land, and my home, after all, was down in Maryland, because my father, my mother, my brothers, my sisters, and friends were there. But I was free and *they should be free!*"

Harriet resolved she would make a home for her family in the North. "...And the Lord helping, I would bring them all here," she once said.

Harriet decided to settle in Philadelphia, at least for a time. The city awed her. She had never seen tall buildings before. There were people everywhere. The streets were filled with the clatter of horses and wagons.

It took time for Harriet to get used to the city and the fast pace of life there. She missed her family. She thought of them often. It saddened her to think that they still lived lives of great hardship.

Harriet got a job in a hotel kitchen. She cooked, washed dishes, and scrubbed pots. She saved almost every cent she earned.

Philadelphia, Harriet soon learned, was a center of abolitionist activity. The abolitionists felt that slavery was wicked. Leaders of the movement included William Lloyd Garrison and Frederick Douglass. Garrison, who was white, had founded an antislavery newspaper called *The Liberator*. He also helped to organize the American Anti-Slavery Society. Douglass, an escaped slave, published *The North Star*, another abolitionist newspaper. Like other abolitionists, Garrison and Douglass often attacked slavery in public speeches.

Harriet also became aware of the work of the

William Lloyd Garrison (left) was once almost lynched by an angry Boston mob for his abolitionist views. Frederick Douglass (right), an escaped slave like Harriet Tubman, worked tirelessly for the antislavery cause.

members of a Christian church known as Quakers. The Quakers were important to the antislavery movement. They sheltered runaway slaves and raised money to support the Underground Railroad. They also wrote and published antislavery books and pamphlets.

Not long after she had settled in Philadelphia, Harriet met William Still, a free black man. He ran a business selling coal. Still helped to manage the Philadelphia Vigilance Committee. The committee

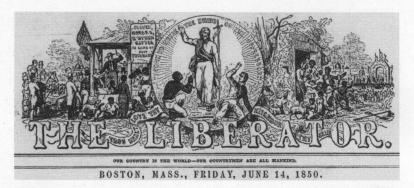

William Lloyd Garrison founded the antislavery newspaper, The Liberator, *in 1831. He continued to publish it until slavery ended in 1865.*

helped runaway slaves find food, clothing, and shelter.

Harriet often visited the office of the Vigilance Committee. There she met and talked with runaways. One night she was there when a stranger arrived. He needed help, he said, in rescuing a black woman and her two children from Cambridge, Maryland.

Harriet listened as the visitor explained that the woman's husband was a free black. His wife and two children were slaves. They would soon be auctioned off at the Cambridge slave market.

The visitor said that a local Quaker might be able to transport the family from Cambridge to Baltimore by boat. But someone was needed to guide the family from Baltimore to Philadelphia and freedom.

The visitor then mentioned the name of the free husband. It was John Bowley. *John Bowley!* Harriet could hardly believe her ears. John Bowley was the name of her brother-in-law, the husband of her sister Mary Ann.

Harriet jumped to her feet and announced that she should be the one to lead the Bowley family to safety. Still didn't like that idea. Harriet was a fugitive herself. Slave hunters in Baltimore would be looking for her.

But Harriet insisted. Still was quick to realize that nothing he could say was going to prevent Harriet from taking part in the rescue mission.

Meanwhile, John Bowley and a Quaker friend had been busy. They were successful in freeing Mary Ann and the two children from the slave pen in Cambridge. Once they were free, John Bowley's friend hid them in his attic.

*In Philadelphia, William Still befriended Harriet Tubman. Born free,
Still helped operate the Philadelphia Vigilance Committee, which did
much to aid runaway slaves.*

One night after dark, the friend led the Bowleys
to a dock at the nearby Choptank River. A small
boat waited there. That night the boat sailed west
into Chesapeake Bay, then north to Baltimore. A
white woman met the boat there. After the Bowleys
were concealed in a wagon loaded with potatoes and
onions, the woman drove to a brick house.

The white woman knocked at the door. "Who's there?" a voice answered.

"A friend with friends," the woman replied.

The door flew open. Harriet rushed forward and threw her arms around her sister.

The Bowleys and Harriet stayed in Baltimore for several days. Then Harriet led the family out of Baltimore. They all followed the Underground Railroad north and east from one station to the next. Sometimes they traveled by foot. Other times, they rode in wagons, hidden under blankets or straw. A boat carried them across the Susquehanna River. At last, Harriet and the Bowleys crossed into the free state of Pennsylvania.

Harriet felt proud that she had been able to guide the Bowleys to safety.

The mission marked the beginning of her long career as a conductor on the Underground Railroad.

THE TRACKLESS TRAIL

AT ABOUT THE SAME TIME THAT Harriet became a conductor on the Underground Railroad, guiding slaves to freedom in the North, Congress passed laws that made her rescue efforts more difficult and dangerous. They were known as the fugitive slave laws. They became effective in 1850.

Runaway slaves living in the North could now be captured. They could then be sent back to their owners in the South. Those captured could not defend themselves. They were not even allowed to have a jury trial.

The laws also dealt harshly with people who

helped the runaways. They could be subject to fines and prison sentences. Federal commissioners were named to enforce the laws.

Like other former slaves, Harriet now faced a life of danger. She could be arrested at any time and taken back to Bucktown.

But the new laws did nothing to change Harriet's mind about rescuing the rest of her family. She did have to reshape her plans, however. Her runaways were no longer safe in Philadelphia or any other northern city. Harriet now had to guide her passengers all the way to Canada.

"No longer," Harriet declared, "could I trust Uncle Sam with my people."

During the summer of 1850, Harriet worked in a hotel in Cape May, New Jersey. She carefully saved the money she earned. She needed it to buy food and supplies for another trip into the South. This time her goal was to bring her husband back north with her.

Harriet still loved John Tubman, even though she

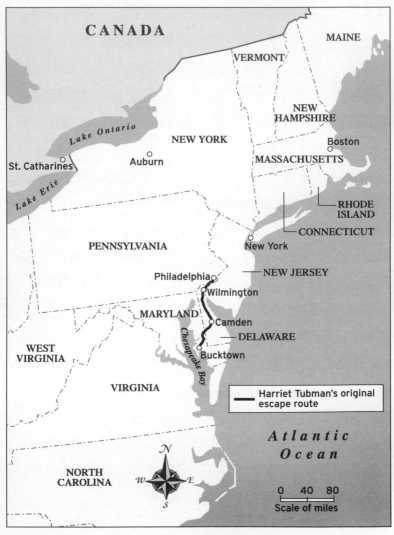

When the fugitive slave laws were passed, Harriet had to lengthen her Underground Railroad route by hundreds of miles. She had to lead runaways to St. Catharines, Ontario, Canada.

had not seen him for two years. She clung to the dream that one day they would live together in freedom in the North.

For the trip south, Harriet wore men's clothing as a disguise. A wide-brimmed felt hat hid the scar on her forehead.

Harriet arrived in the Bucktown area not long after dark one evening. She went directly to her husband's cabin. She had no idea what he would do when he saw her.

She knocked at the door. John answered. He stared at what he took to be a short man in rumpled clothing.

Harriet held out her hands to him. "John, it's me," she said. "It's Harriet."

Then Harriet saw that John was not alone. An attractive young woman was sitting by the fireplace. She got up and walked to the door to stand next to John.

"I've come back for you, John," Harriet said.

John looked at Harriet in disbelief. "This is Caroline," he said in a quiet voice, indicating the woman at his side. "She's my wife now. I'm not going north or any other place."

Harriet stared at John and the woman for a moment. Then she turned without a word and departed. Later that night, she left Bucktown with several slaves who wanted to escape.

Harriet never saw John Tubman again. But she never stopped caring for him. Even though their marriage had ended, she carried his name for the rest of her life. She was deeply saddened when, years later, she heard of his death.

With each journey into the South, Harriet became more and more confident in her role as a conductor. She knew her escape route well. She was aware of the hiding places she could use. She had a network of friends that she could depend upon.

She would strike quickly and by surprise. Often she and her fugitives would begin their long trip north on a Saturday night. Sunday was a day of rest. With luck, her runaways would not be missed until Monday morning.

Harriet's journey north from Maryland into

Fern Cunningham created this dramatic sculptural representation of Harriet Tubman and a band of runaways for Harriet Tubman Park in Boston. Titled "Step on Board," the sculpture was dedicated in 1999.

Canada stretched 650 miles. St. Catharines, in the Canadian province of Ontario, was her final stop. At Salem Church in St. Catharines, Harriet gave thanks for a successful journey.

During the winter, St. Catharines was often bitterly cold. Sometimes those who Harriet had rescued would grumble about the snow, ice, and frigid temperatures. Winters in Maryland had been relatively mild.

One night, Harriet and a group of runaways were huddled about the fireplace in her home. Throughout the evening, Harriet kept hearing complaints of how the freezing temperatures and chill wind stung their faces and numbed their fingers and toes.

Harriet finally decided that she had heard enough. "It's warm in Maryland," she said, "nice and warm down there compared to here. You want to go back there?"

All were silent for a moment. Then one by one the runaways answered "No."

Harriet would surely have been surprised if

anyone had answered yes. As she once noted, "I've seen hundreds and hundreds of slaves who finally got to the North and freedom. But I never yet saw one who was willing to go back South and be a slave."

CHAPTER 9

A WOMAN CALLED MOSES

DURING THE EARLY YEARS OF THE 1850s, Harriet's life settled into a carefully planned routine. She rented a house in St. Catharines where she spent the winters. Several former slaves moved in with her. They chopped wood and did other jobs to earn money.

When spring arrived, Harriet would journey to Philadelphia or Cape May, New Jersey. She would spend the summer cooking or cleaning in hotels. She made two trips into the South each year to bring slaves north. The money she earned during the summer helped to pay for these missions.

The Underground Railroad aided Harriet. She

was also helped by her deep religious faith. Once Harriet and her band of fugitives entered a town. In the town was a station on the Underground Railroad. When they reached the house, Harriet knocked on the door. There was no answer. She rapped a second time. Still no answer. Harriet sensed there was something wrong.

When Harriet rapped a third time, a window on the first floor was thrust open. The head of a white man appeared.

"Who are you?" he asked. "What do you want?"

Harriet asked for the stationmaster. The man said that the stationmaster was not there. He had been forced to flee for helping runaways.

Harriet feared the man might sound the alarm. She told her charges they must hide. On the edge of the town, she knew of a small island in a swamp where they could go.

She led the runaways into the swamp. When they reached the island, she ordered them to lie down in the tall grass. Cold, wet, and hungry, some of the runaways began to whimper.

Harriet prayed, confident the Lord would come to their aid.

Not long before nightfall, a man came walking slowly along a pathway at the swamp's edge. He was dressed as a Quaker, wearing a dark suit and broad-brimmed hat. He seemed to be talking to himself. Harriet strained to hear what he was saying.

"My wagon stands in the barnyard of the farm across the way," she heard him say. "The horse is in the stable. The harness hangs on the wall." Then the man was gone.

That night Harriet and her runaways made their way to the farm. They found the wagon, horse, and harness. The wagon was loaded with food. Harriet and the fugitives had been saved.

Harriet didn't believe what had happened was strange. Throughout her life she believed all of her prayers would be answered.

After Harriet had made several trips to the South, slaves began calling her Moses. Moses was one of the most important figures in the Bible. He led his people out of slavery in Egypt. Then he brought

St. Louis-born artist Frederic Jean Thalinger, who worked in wood, stone, and soap, created this sculpture of a strong and resolute Harriet Tubman.

them to Canaan, the Promised Land. Harriet was like Moses because she led her enslaved people out of the South to freedom in the North.

Slave owners began hearing tales of Moses. At first, they did not know that Harriet Tubman and Moses were the same person. When they learned the truth, they printed posters offering big rewards for Harriet "Moses" Tubman.

Harriet was once sitting in a railroad station in the South waiting for a train. She overheard two men talking about her. They were trying to make up their minds whether she was the woman pictured on a wanted poster on the station wall.

Harried tried to stay calm. She had been carrying a book. Now she opened the book and stared at a page of text as if she were reading it.

One of the men shook his head. "No," he said, "that can't be her. The one they want can't read."

Harriet breathed a quiet sigh of relief.

In 1857, Harriet decided to settle in Auburn, New York. A small town in the central part of the state about fifteen miles west of Syracuse, Auburn was an important station on the Underground Railroad.

U.S. Senator William Seward, an abolitionist, helped Harriet to acquire what was to be her new home. Seward was a friend and admirer of Harriet's. Seward was the governor of New York from 1839 to 1842. He later served as U.S. Secretary of State.

No cash was needed for the purchase. But Harriet was required to make small monthly payments. She would live in the house for most of the rest of her life.

Harriet was at her home in Auburn in 1857 when she was brought troubling news. Her father had been arrested for trying to help a slave escape. Ben was now more than seventy years old. Harriet knew that he would be severely punished if he were found guilty. Harriet wasted no time in making plans to head south. So began one of the most dramatic rescues of her career.

She arrived in Bucktown late one night. Without

Governor William H. Seward of New York was a close friend of Harriet Tubman's. He arranged for her to purchase a home for herself on his property.

any advance notice, she slipped into the cabin of her astonished parents. She told them to prepare for a trip.

But Harriet could see she had a problem. Her passengers were usually young and strong. They were able to walk long distances and put up with many hardships. Harriet's parents were in their seventies. They moved slowly and stiffly. They could not walk to freedom. They would have to ride.

From a nearby farm, Harriet kidnapped an old horse. She got an axle, then fitted boards over it for her parents to sit on.

Thomas Garrett's Delaware home was a stop on the Underground Railroad. He wrote, "She got her parents . . . on this rude vehicle . . . and drove to town in a style no human being ever did before or since."

Within three days, Harriet and her parents had arrived in Wilmington, Delaware. "Next day, I furnished them with money to take them all to Canada," Thomas Garrett wrote. "I afterwards sold the horse, and sent them the balance of the proceeds."

Harriet and her parents spent the winter in St. Catharines. In the spring, she moved them to her home in Auburn.

In December 1860, Harriet made her final rescue

The Cyrus Gates house in Broome County, New York, was a station on the Underground Railroad. A secret space under the roof could be used as a hiding place in emergencies.

mission. It was just four months before the Civil War began. Her last trip was more dangerous than any that had gone before.

Thomas Garrett knew of Harriet's journey. "There is much more risk on the road than there has been for several months past," Garrett wrote in a letter to William Still. "Yet . . . Harriet seems to have had a special angel to guard her on her journey of mercy."

Harriet and her last group of runaways arrived safely in Philadelphia. Then they traveled on to Canada.

Harriet made a total of nineteen trips into the South and back. These rescue missions brought freedom to nearly three hundred slaves. At one time, slave owners offered as much as $40,000 in reward money to anyone who could bring them Harriet "Moses" Tubman, dead or alive. But she was never caught. She was a great symbol of hope to any slave who dreamed of freedom.

CHAPTER 10

GENERAL TUBMAN

DURING THE WINTER OF 1857–1858, Harriet was living in St. Catharines with her parents, Ben and Rit. During that time, she kept having a troubling dream. Harriet was, as she described it, "in a wilderness sort of place, all full of rocks and bushes."

In her dream, the head of a snake appeared among the rocks. Harriet stared at it in horror. Then the head changed, becoming the head of a man with a long white beard and fiery gray-blue eyes. The man would not take his eyes off her.

Then two other heads appeared beside the man's head. These were the heads of younger men. Suddenly, a great mob of men rushed in to swarm over the rocks. They struck down the heads of the young men and then the head of the old man.

Harriet had the strange dream again and again. What upset her about it was the way the old man kept his gaze fixed upon her. "He was," she said, "wishful like, just as if he was going to speak to me."

The dream disturbed Harriet. She thought about it many times as she tended to her parents and prepared to move with them to her home in Auburn.

In the spring of 1858, abolitionist Reverend J.W. Loguen brought a white man to St. Catharines to meet Harriet. His name was John Brown.

Harriet looked at the man and gasped. His was the face of the old, bearded man with the blazing eyes in her dream.

Harriet was puzzled. What did it all mean?

The fifty-nine-year-old Brown was well known. He was an abolitionist who favored drastic action to destroy slavery. "God's angry man," he was called.

Born in 1800 in Torrington, Connecticut, Brown

John Brown was in his mid-fifties and heavily bearded when he asked Harriet Tubman to join him in his antislavery crusade.

was raised in Ohio. He had risked his life to guide runaway slaves across the Ohio River to freedom.

In 1855, Brown followed several of his sons and settled in Kansas. At the time, the Kansas Territory was deeply troubled. Southern settlers were seeking to establish Kansas as a slave state. Abolitionists and many religious groups wanted to keep Kansas free. Bloody clashes between the two sides were common.

In May 1856, proslavery settlers attacked and burned the town of Lawrence, Kansas. Brown was furious. In revenge, Brown led a group of men to a settlement on Pottawatomie Creek. There he and his men murdered five proslavery men.

In the months that followed, Brown lived as an outlaw. He still had many abolitionist supporters who were eager to help him.

When Harriet met Brown, he told her of his plans. He wanted to take up arms and free huge numbers of slaves. He was even considering an invasion of the South. He would strike first at Harpers Ferry, Virginia (now West Virginia).

Brown asked for Harriet's help. He wanted to know the routes she had used to bring slaves out of Maryland. He wanted her to tell him the names of places where she and her fugitives had hidden and the names of people who had helped her.

He needed this information, Brown said, because

Washington, D.C.'s massive Israel African Methodist Church, now the Metropolitan AME Church, is known to have offered shelter to runaways. The funeral of Frederick Douglass was held there in 1895.

he wanted runaways by the thousands to join him at Harpers Ferry.

Harriet was cautious. She knew Brown had been violent in the past.

Still Harriet could not help but be stirred by Brown. He hated slavery as much as she did. He wanted to put slavery to a sudden end. Harriet agreed to help him.

Brown was impressed by Harriet. He liked her spirit and resolve. While still in St. Catharines, he wrote a letter to his son, praising her. In the letter, he referred to her as "General Tubman."

In the fall of 1858, Harriet traveled to Boston. Her friends in New York had urged her to go there. Abolitionists in Boston were eager to meet her.

Harriet felt safer in Boston than in most cities of the North. The fugitive slave laws were not always enforced there.

Soon Harriet made a speech before an antislavery group. In her husky voice, she told of the trips she had made into the South. She described the slaves who she had chosen to come north with her. Her audience listened as she told how they traveled on foot, hiding in barns and haystacks during the day. Harriet also explained how stationmasters had offered her and her runaways food and shelter. She told of their great joy in reaching Canada.

Her audience listened in awe. When she had finished, they stood and clapped and cheered.

The great success of her speech sparked a new

career for Harriet. She became a popular speaker. She visited such Massachusetts towns and cities as Concord, Framingham, and Worcester to speak against slavery.

During the fall and winter in Boston, Harriet met with John Brown a number of times. She told him of the routes that she had taken out of the South. She described the hiding places that she had used. She even drew maps for him.

During the spring and summer of 1859, Harriet and Brown were out of touch. No doubt she expected to hear from him. But she did not.

Harriet had once suggested to Brown that he strike on July 4. This is the anniversary of American independence. But July 4, 1859, came and went, and nothing happened.

Then Harriet fell ill. She was exhausted. The head wound she had suffered as a child troubled her, too. But slowly she got better. On October 17, 1859, Harriet was in New York City, visiting friends. At breakfast that morning, a troubled look crossed her face. "Something's wrong," she said. "Something dreadful has happened, or is about to happen."

She closed her eyes and bowed her head, then spoke again. "It's Captain Brown. Something has happened to him."

The next day's newspapers told the story. John Brown had gathered a band of twenty-two men, sixteen of them white. They had seized the U.S. storehouse for guns and ammunition at Harpers Ferry. But the local militia soon attacked Brown and

John Brown (center, with rifle over his shoulder) sets out for Harpers Ferry with his loyal band of followers.

his men. Then a company of U.S. Marines joined the battle.

Ten of Brown's men fell dead, including two of his sons. Brown was captured. Tried in court for treason, he was found guilty and hanged in December 1859.

Harriet was horrified by these events. She recalled the dream that she kept having about the three heads. Now she understood. The heads in her dream represented Brown and his two sons.

The tragedy at Harpers Ferry deeply moved Harriet. She was willing to risk her life for her people. But she thought nothing could be nobler than for a white man to do it.

Harriet applauded John Brown for his great courage for as long as she lived. She hailed him for doing more than anyone else to deliver slaves out of bondage.

CHAPTER 11

RESCUE IN TROY

AFTER THE EXCITEMENT AT HARPERS Ferry, Harriet returned to Auburn to spend a few quiet months. In the spring of 1860, she was asked to attend an antislavery meeting in Boston. On the way, she stopped in Troy, New York, to visit her cousin. One of the stormiest events of her life would happen there.

While in Troy, Harriet learned of a runaway slave named Charles Nalle. He was about thirty years old, tall, and good-looking. Nalle had been arrested as a fugitive slave and taken to the local courthouse to be tried. If found guilty, Nalle could be sent back to Virginia and slavery.

On the day of the trial, Harriet set out for the courtroom. The streets surrounding the courthouse were filled with many people. Some were abolitionists. They talked of freeing Nalle. Others were proslavery. They demanded that Nalle be put aboard the first train to the South.

Despite the crowd, Harriet made her way to the second floor of the courtroom. The judge had just delivered his decision. Nalle was to be returned to Virginia.

A wagon was waiting in the street to carry off Nalle. But the large, angry crowd worried the marshals. They did not want to bring Nalle outside.

On the far side of the street opposite the courthouse, stood a throng of free blacks. They could see Harriet through the courthouse window. Even from a distance, she could be recognized by the sunbonnet she was wearing.

The crowd kept getting bigger. The whole street was now filled. People pushed, shoved, and shouted.

When Nalle did not appear, some of the free blacks thought they had been tricked. "They've taken him out another way," said one.

"No," said another, looking up through the courtroom window. "There stands Moses yet. As long as she is there, he is safe."

The marshals tried to clear the stairs to the street several times. But the crowd would not budge.

Harriet was one of those blocking the way. "Come, old woman," said one of the marshals. "You must get out of this." But Harriet stubbornly kept her place.

A plan was hatching in her mind. Perhaps Nalle could be snatched away from the authorities and delivered to freedom. It was risky, but worth trying. Even if it failed, Nalle would be no worse off than he was now.

After a long wait, several marshals came down the stairs to make an announcement. If the crowd would clear the stairs and open a path to the wagon, they would bring Nalle down the front way. The crowd agreed.

Nalle was brought down. His wrists were bound. He had guards on either side of him. They brushed past Harriet who was at the bottom of the stairs. She seemed harmless. She was just a small, bent-over, black woman in a sunbonnet.

As soon as Nalle and the marshals went by her, Harriet flew into action. "Here he comes!" she shouted. "Take him!"

With that, she tore into the officers guarding Nalle. She grabbed one and pulled him to the ground. She attacked another with her fists.

At the same time, the crowd pushed forward. Harriet took Nalle by the arm and pulled him along with her. Blows from marshals' clubs rained down on her. But she ignored them.

"A regular battlefield," a local newspaper, the *Troy Whig*, called it, with the surging mass "pulling, hauling, mauling, and shouting."

"Drag us out!" Harriet shouted. "Drag him to the river! Drown him! But don't let them have him!"

Harriet and Nalle were knocked to the ground by one of the marshals. They got up, only to be knocked down again.

With his wrists bound, Nalle was all but helpless.

HERE WAS BEGUN
APRIL 27, 1860
THE RESCUE
OF
CHARLES NALLE
AN
ESCAPED SLAVE WHO HAD BEEN
ARRESTED UNDER THE
FUGITIVE SLAVE ACT

This plaque in Troy, New York, commemorates the escape of Charles Nalle.

Blood streamed from his head. Harriet's clothes were torn. Her shoes were pulled from her feet. But she would not let go of Nalle.

The crowd swept the pair along the streets toward the river. On reaching it, Nalle was put into a rowboat. The rower set out for the opposite shore. Harriet and several hundred others boarded a ferryboat. It followed the rowboat across the river.

The rescue was far from over. Police on the other

side of the river had been alerted by telegraph of Nalle's escape. They were waiting for the rowboat. Grabbing Nalle, they locked him in a house.

Led by Harriet, the crowd rushed to the house. Police guarded the entrance and were posted at every window. Harriet and her followers threw rocks at the police. The police responded with gunfire. The crowd fell back.

Suddenly, a black man broke from the crowd and dashed toward the house. Big and strong, he slammed into the front door with his shoulder and it swung open. A dozen men poured through.

As the mob tried to make its way up the stairs, police fired down. Two men were hit and fell. The others reached the top of the stairs. They burst in upon the startled Nalle. They picked him up and carried him outside.

They put him into a wagon. Suddenly, Nalle was on his way north to Canada and freedom.

Harriet herself was now in danger of arrest because she had helped Nalle to escape. Her friends hid her in a house near Troy.

From Troy, Harriet went to Boston. She met with antislavery groups there.

Could slavery be ended without terrible bloodshed? That was the question on everyone's lips.

Harriet did not think so. "They may say 'Peace, Peace' as much as they like," she declared. "I know there's going to be war."

CHAPTER 12

NURSE, SCOUT, SPY

JOHN BROWN HAD FAILED TO BRING about a slave revolt. But his actions were not forgotten. Many in the North thought he was a hero.

In the South, Brown's actions had caused fear and anger. To many Southerners, John Brown was a madman.

There was anger between the North and South when the presidential election of 1860 took place. Once Abraham Lincoln was elected, things got worse. South Carolina seceded from the United States of America. Early the next year, six more states in the South also withdrew from the Union. The seven rebellious states banded together to form the Confederate States of America.

On April 12, 1861, Confederate guns opened fire on Fort Sumter in the harbor of Charleston, South Carolina. The Civil War had begun.

Harriet was in Canada when the war broke out. She hurried to Boston to be with her abolitionist friends.

The operations of the Underground Railroad came to a halt when the war started. But there were new roles for Harriet to play.

Many abolitionists did not think President Lincoln was doing enough to end slavery. Harriet agreed. "God is ahead of Mr. Lincoln," Harriet said "God won't let Mister Lincoln beat the South until he does the right thing." The "right thing," thought Harriet, was "setting the Negroes free."

In the fall of 1861, the North's Union forces captured Port Royal Island, South Carolina. Owners of the area's rich cotton and rice plantations abandoned their property. Their slaves flooded into the nearby towns of Beaufort and Hilton Head.

Besides being homeless, they were sick and starving. Union military leaders asked for help.

Hundreds of Northerners answered the call. Harriet was one of those who responded. Governor John A. Andrews of Massachusetts paved the way for Harriet's journey into the South. He arranged for her to be assigned to the headquarters of General Isaac Ingalls Stevens.

Harriet arrived in Beaufort, South Carolina, in March 1862. She was surprised that she was not able to talk easily with the local blacks. They spoke Gullah. Gullah is a dialect made up of many words native to the African nation of Angola. "Why, their language down there in the far South is just as different from ours in Maryland as you can think," Harriet said. "They laughed when they heard me talk, and I could not understand them."

That wasn't Harriet's only problem. The local black people did not trust whites. They were also suspicious of those who, like Harriet, worked for whites. Harriet struggled to gain their confidence. In time, Harriet formed a strong bond with them. She

When Union forces captured Port Royal Island, South Carolina (in background), hundreds of plantation slaves gained their freedom. Harriet Tubman traveled to South Carolina to care for the sick and injured among them.

listened to their complaints. She learned their needs. Then she would meet with military leaders and seek their help.

Harriet also worked as a nurse. Her patients included white soldiers wounded in the field. She also treated blacks who had fled the plantations

Near Newbern, North Carolina, slaves leave their masters to join Northern forces.

where they had once worked. Some were ill. Others were on the brink of starvation.

After the war, in an interview with Sarah Bradford, Harriet described what it was like. "I'd go to the hospital early every morning. I'd get a big chunk of ice and put it in a basin, and fill it with water. Then I'd take a sponge and begin. First man I'd come to, I'd thrash away the flies, and they'd rise, like bees around a hive. Then I'd begin to bathe their wounds, and by the time I'd bathed three or four [soldiers], the fire and heat would have melted the ice and made the water warm, and it would be as red as clear blood. Then I'd go and get more ice, and by the time I got back to the next one, the flies would be around the first ones [as] black and thick as ever."

On September 22, 1862, President Lincoln issued the Emancipation Proclamation. The document said that all slaves within the Confederate states would become free on January 1, 1863. Of course, the federal government had no means of enforcing the proclamation in the South. Yet the document offered slaves in the South the promise of freedom once the war ended.

The Emancipation Proclamation also stated that blacks "will be received in the armed service of the United States." They could now fight in the Union Army.

In the months that followed, Harriet showed her strong military spirit. In the spring of 1863, Harriet was asked to lead a small unit of black troops behind enemy lines. She returned with important information about Confederate forces in the area. She reported the number of enemy troops. She told where they were camped and how they were armed. Sometimes she carried a musket. Afterward, Harriet was hailed for "displaying remarkable courage, zeal, and fidelity."

During most operations, the forty-two-year-old Harriet wore a dark blue coat over a striped wool dress. She wore her familiar bandanna, too.

On some missions, Harriet is known to have worn "bloomers." The bloomer outfit took the form of a short skirt over loose trousers that fitted tightly and buttoned at the ankle. To Harriet, these were simply pants.

Harriet's most noted military assignment took place in the summer of 1863. General David Hunter, who commanded Union forces in the South, asked for her help.

General Hunter's mission required Harriet to join him as he took three steam-powered gunboats up the Combahee River in South Carolina. The

During the Civil War, freed African Americans by the thousands aided the Union cause as laborers, wagon drivers, and hospital workers. This is a scene at the Quartermaster's Wharf in Alexandria, Virginia.

purpose of the expedition was to blow up mines that had been placed in the river by the rebels. They were also to destroy bridges and railroads. Colonel James Montgomery was named to head the mission.

Hundreds of former slaves were known to be in the area. General Hunter wanted Harriet to lead them to safety.

The gunboats made their way up the Combahee. Groups of curious slaves left the rice fields in which they had been working to line the banks on both sides of the river. Harriet had never seen anything like it.

She later described the scene. "One woman brought two pigs, a white one and a black one. We took them on board. [We] named the white pig Beauregard [after Confederate general Pierre P. T. Beauregard] and the black pig Jeff Davis [for Jefferson Davis, president of the Confederacy].

"Sometimes the women would come with twins hanging around their necks. Appears like I never saw so many twins in my life; bags on their shoulders, baskets on their heads, and young ones tagging behind..."

To rescue the hundreds of fugitives, rowboats were sent from the warships to the shore. The former slaves made a great rush to get into the boats. Even after the boats were filled, others tried to get in. When the boats pulled from the shore, some refugees clung to the sides. Feeling that they might go under, the men rowing struck out at the former slaves with their oars.

Harriet Tubman is not believed to have used a musket during the Civil War, but she was known to carry one.

Colonel Montgomery was watching from the deck of one of the gunboats. He became alarmed. He turned to Harriet, hoping she could restore peace.

"Moses," he said, "you'll have to give them a song."

At once, Harriet's low-pitched, throaty voice drifted over the scene. She sang:

Of the whole creation in the East or in the West,
The glorious Yankee nation is the greatest and
     the best.
Come along! Come along! Don't be alarmed,
Uncle Sam is rich enough to give you all a farm.

The crowd calmed. Once each rowboat unloaded its passengers, it returned to shore for more. Eventually, close to eight hundred people were brought to safety.

CHAPTER 13

RETURN HOME

H ARRIET WORKED FOR THE UNION cause from 1862 until the war ended in 1865. During that time, she saw the Union attack on Fort Wagner. Fort Wagner guarded the entrance to the harbor of Charleston, South Carolina.

The attack was led by the 54th Massachusetts, the first black regiment organized in the North. The free blacks that made up the regiment wore spotless uniforms. They carried the newest weapons. They were led by Colonel Robert G. Shaw, a twenty-six-year-old white officer.

At dusk on July 18, 1863, the order came to attack. Shot and shell rained down on the black regiment as they advanced across an open beach toward the fort. They held the fort for a short time. But they had to fall back in the face of heavy gunfire.

More than 350 black soldiers were killed, wounded, or captured at Fort Wagner. Colonel Shaw was among those who died.

Fort Wagner marked the first important use of black troops during the war. Before the battle, some Northerners had expressed doubts about the courage of black troops. After the battle, there were no more doubts.

When the fighting ended, Harriet helped nurse the wounded and bury the dead. Years later, she spoke with great feeling about the role she had played: "...We saw the lightning, and that was the guns; and then we heard thunder, and that was the big guns; and then we heard the rain falling, and that was drops of blood falling. And when we came to get in the crops, it was dead men that we reaped."

On April 9, 1865, General Robert E. Lee surrendered to General Ulysses S. Grant at

Appomattox Court House, Virginia. The Civil War was over.

For black Americans in the South, Lee's surrender was a great victory. They now had freedom—what they always wanted.

That summer, Harriet made plans to return to her Auburn, New York, home. She boarded a train in Washington, D.C., for the trip north. When the conductor asked for her ticket, Harriet handed him a military pass. She had been given it for her work as a nurse. The pass entitled her to travel at half the regular price.

The conductor looked at the pass. He scowled. "Come hustle out of here," he ordered. Then he called Harriet an insulting name. He said that people of her color were not entitled to travel at a reduced rate.

Harriet protested. The conductor grabbed her by the arm. "I'll make you tired of trying to stay here," he declared.

Harriet tried to resist. The conductor called other men to help him. Together they dragged Harriet out

This photograph of Harriet Tubman is likely to have been taken after her return to Auburn. Her face and hands show evidence of her life of labor and hardship.

of the car. The train's white passengers watched. Nobody said or did anything to help her. The conductor and his men pushed and shoved Harriet into the baggage car. In the struggle, Harriet's arm was badly sprained.

As the train rolled north, Harriet must have felt saddened and confused by the strange turn of events. She had worked without pay for three years for "the glorious Yankee nation." She had dodged bullets and cannon fire. Now she was returning home, forced to ride in a dark and dismal baggage car, with a bruised and aching arm.

FINAL YEARS

ARRIET WAS IN HER MID-FORTIES when she settled down in her home in Auburn.

She was exhausted from her years of war service. The incident on the train had left her badly hurt. She was also penniless. Old Ben and Rit, her aged parents, looked to her for support.

Harriet's energy never lessened. She planted apple trees and worked in her large vegetable garden. Friends and neighbors helped to provide her with money, food, and clothing.

Whatever she had, Harriet shared with those less fortunate. She offered food and shelter to poor blacks that passed through Auburn in search of jobs and homes. She began raising money to benefit schools for freed slaves in the South.

Harriet also spent time trying to collect her pay. She had not been paid for her work as nurse, scout, and spy. Her requests for the money went unanswered.

Harriet asked her old friend William H. Seward to help her. Seward was U.S. Secretary of State at the

The rebuilt Harriet Tubman Home in Auburn, New York. It was opened to the public in 1953. The original home, which housed the poor and needy, was torn down in 1944.

time. He asked Congress to act on Harriet's behalf. Harriet's other friends did the same. But nothing happened. The debt was never paid.

It was Sarah Bradford who helped ease Harriet's money problems. In the spring of 1868, Bradford began writing the story of Harriet's life. Published in 1869, the biography was titled *Scenes in the Life of Harriet Tubman.*

Sarah Bradford received $1,200 when she sold the book to a publisher. She gave the money to Harriet. It was a large sum of money for the time. Harriet was able to pay her most pressing debts. "There's cider in the cellar," said a jubilant Harriet, "and the black folks, they'll have some...."

Harriet spent some of the money on the education of black children in the South. She also continued to assist those who appeared at her door needing help.

In 1869, someone from Harriet's past visited her. His name was Nelson Davis. Harriet had met him at a South Carolina army post during the war. Davis had seen battlefield action with the 8th U.S.

This photograph was taken around 1885. Harriet Tubman Davis (far left) poses with her husband, Nelson Davis (third from left), and residents of the Harriet Tubman Home in Auburn, New York.

Colored Infantry Volunteers. He was about twenty years younger than Harriet.

Before many days passed, Davis asked Harriet to marry him. Harriet accepted. Her first husband, John Tubman, had died two years earlier.

An Auburn newspaper, in its issue of March 19, 1869, reported on the wedding: "Before a large and very select audience Harriet Tubman...took unto herself a husband and made one [Nelson Davis] a happy man. Both born slaves...they stood there, last evening, *free*, and were joined as man and wife."

Davis was tall, handsome, and appeared healthy. But when he was in the Army, he had come down with tuberculosis, a disease of the lungs. Davis became sicker as time passed. Harriet spent a good part of her married life nursing her husband. Nelson Davis died in 1888.

During her years in retirement, Harriet was an enthusiastic supporter of Susan B. Anthony. Along with Elizabeth Cady Stanton, Anthony campaigned to give women the right to vote.

Harriet admired Anthony. She attended Anthony's lectures many times.

One such lecture took place at a Rochester, New York, church during the 1880s. After she had finished speaking, Anthony looked out upon the audience. "Friends," she said, "we have in the audience that wonderful woman, Harriet Tubman, from whom we would like to hear, if she will kindly come to the platform."

The people turned toward Harriet and grinned at

Harriet Tubman was strong in her support of women's rights activists Susan B. Anthony (left) and Elizabeth Cady Stanton (right).

what they saw. The church was warm and Harriet was tired. She had fallen asleep. It took several minutes to wake her.

Harriet slowly made her way up the aisle and onto the stage. "Ladies," said Anthony, "I am glad to present to you Harriet Tubman, the conductor of the Underground Railroad."

"Yes, ladies," Harriet began, "I was the conductor of the Underground Railroad for eight years, and I can say what most conductors can't say—I never ran my train off the track and I never lost a passenger." The audience laughed and applauded.

One day in 1896, Harriet heard that a large piece of land across the road from her house was to be sold at auction. The property had two houses on it. Harriet had long eyed the property. It would be a perfect home for the sick and needy.

Harriet did not have the money to buy the land. But she was determined to have it. She decided to go to the auction and bid.

She later told what happened: "They were all white folks there but me, and I was there like a blackberry in a pail of milk, but I hid down in a corner, and no one knew who was bidding. The man began down pretty low, and I kept going up by fifties. At last I got up to fourteen hundred and fifty. And then others stopped bidding, and the man said, 'All done. Who is the buyer?'

"'Harriet Tubman,' I shouted."

Harriet went to a local bank and borrowed the money to pay for the property. She used the property itself as security for the loan.

Making the monthly loan payments was difficult for Harriet. In 1903, she turned the land over to the African Methodist Episcopal Zion Church of Auburn. Harriet had worshipped at the church for years.

The church built a center on the property to care for the poor, sick, and needy. A longtime dream of Harriet's was thus fulfilled.

But Harriet became unhappy with the way the church ran the home. Harriet had taken in strangers for years. She never asked them for money. But the church asked people who wanted to live in the home to pay a fee.

"When I gave the home over to the Zion Church, what do you suppose they did?" said Harriet. "Why, they made a rule that nobody could come in without one hundred dollars. What's the good of a home if a person who wants to get in has to have money?"

This is probably the last photograph taken of Harriet Tubman. In 1911, an article in The New York World said of her: "Now with the weight of almost a hundred years on her shoulders, she awaits the last call."

Harriet and the church eventually came to a friendly settlement. Harriet herself moved into the house in 1911.

At the age of ninety-two, Harriet became confined to her bed. She still had many visitors, however. One was Mary B. Talbert, head of the New York State Federation of Colored Women's Clubs.

Harriet was aware that Talbert and her organization were active in the struggle to win the right for women to vote. Harriet had a message for these women. "Stand together," she said.

Not many weeks later, on March 10, 1913, Harriet died of pneumonia. She was about ninety-three.

One of her brothers, William Henry, and a few of her friends were at her bedside. They held hands and sang one of Harriet's favorite songs, "Swing Low, Sweet Chariot."

Harriet would not allow herself to be left out of the ceremony.

She uttered a few words to draw her loved ones closer. Then, with feeble hands, she gently directed the chorus until death claimed her.

HARRIET TUBMAN REMEMBERED

O N JUNE 12, 1914, ABOUT A YEAR after Harriet's death, the people of Auburn, New York, organized a day in her tribute. Bands played. Flags flew from public buildings. A bronze plaque in her honor was unveiled. It saluted her for her "rare courage."

At the Auburn Auditorium, several notable people spoke. Each hailed Harriet for her many achievements.

One of the speakers was Booker T. Washington, a famous black educator. He praised Harriet as the woman who "had brought the two races nearer together."

The bronze plaque in Auburn is just one of the

This Auburn, New York, plaque in Harriet Tubman's memory was dedicated in 1914, a year after her death.

many memorials in Harriet Tubman's honor. Many schools and public buildings have been named for her. Dozens of articles and books have been written about "the Moses of her people."

Artists have painted her likeness. Sculptors have preserved her image in wood, stone, and metal.

In Auburn, New York, the African Methodist Episcopal Zion Church has been active in keeping Harriet Tubman's name alive. The Harriet Tubman Home, the two-story wood-frame building that served the poor, was torn down in 1944. The church had the structure rebuilt. It now stands as a memorial to Harriet's life and work.

Many thousands of people visit the home each year. A library and large assembly hall have been added to the site.

Some memorials to Harriet Tubman were established even before her passing. The Harriet Tubman House in Boston is one.

Founded in 1891, the Harriet Tubman House took in young African-American female boarders.

Most of them were from the South. Other places of lodging were closed to them because of their race. The Harriet Tubman House gave them food, clothing, and a chance for friendships.

Harriet Tubman

Black Heritage USA 13c

This United States postage stamp honoring Harriet Tubman was issued in 1978.

Harriet visited the home in 1909, four years before her death. The Harriet Tubman House is now part of the United South End Settlements in Boston.

In New York City, Harriet Tubman is remembered by the Harriet Tubman Learning Center. The center offers classroom instruction for needy children. New York is also home to the Harriet Tubman Family Living Center, a shelter for homeless families.

Cleveland, Ohio, offers the Harriet Tubman Museum. It displays materials relating to African-American history.

Much has been done in recent years to preserve

Underground Railroad sites. Many stations were in poor condition. In 1990, Congress called upon the National Park Service to begin preservation work.

Travelers will eventually be able to follow a driving tour from one restored site to the next. Tour guides will explain the historic importance of each. In some cases, the guides may be descendants of fugitive slaves. There are dozens of Underground Railroad sites that can be visited today.

It's exciting to visit these sites or follow a section of the Railroad. In some cases, the terrain is not much different from what it was one hundred and fifty years ago. You get a fresh sense of history in retracing the footsteps of the runaways.

Harriet Tubman was a rare and remarkable woman. She was strong, brave, and determined. She was a person of deep spiritual faith.

She sought no personal gain. She wanted no glory.

How would she have felt about the many Harriet

Judith Bryant d'Oronzio at the grave of her great-great-aunt, Harriet Tubman, in Auburn, New York.

Tubman monuments and memorials, about the schools and other institutions named for her?

What would she have thought about the books, the paintings, and the sculptures created in her honor?

How would she have reacted?

Judith Bryant d'Oronzio, Harriet Tubman's great-

great-grandniece, who lives in Auburn, New York, was once asked that question.

"She was a humble woman," d'Oronzio noted. "She had simple ways.

"All the tributes may have been troubling to her," d'Oronzio continued. "She might not like the idea of so much money being spent to honor her. I think she would have preferred that it be spent to provide food or shelter for people in need.

"During her life, she shared what she had. She rarely spent money on herself. She devoted herself to helping others. I'm sure she would display that same generosity of spirit today."

CHRONOLOGY

1820 or
 1821   Harriet Tubman is born.

1835   Suffers a life-threatening blow to the head.

1844   Marries John Tubman.

1849   Escapes from slavery into Pennsylvania.

1850   Makes first of nineteen trips into the South to
        rescue slaves.

1852   Moves to St. Catharines, Ontario, Canada.

1857   Aids parents in escaping from slavery; settles in
        Auburn, New York.

1858   Meets John Brown, noted abolitionist.

1861–65 Serves as a nurse, scout, and spy for Union forces
        during the Civil War.

1869   Marries Nelson Davis.

1888   Nelson Davis dies.

1913   (March 10) Harriet Tubman dies in Auburn,
        New York.

BIBLIOGRAPHY

Primary Sources

Bradford, Sarah H. *Harriet: The Moses of Her People*. New York: George R. Lockwood & Son, 1886.

Electronic edition available from the Academic Affairs Library, University of North Carolina.

Web site: www.metalab.unc.edu/docsouth/harriet/harriet.html

Secondary Sources

Blockson, Charles L. *Hippocrene Guide to the Underground Railroad*. New York: Hippocrene Books, 1994.

Conrad, Earl. *Harriet Tubman*. Washington, D.C.: Associated Publishers, 1943.

FURTHER READING

Bentley, Judith. *"Dear Friend," Thomas Garrett & William Still; Collaborators on the Underground Railroad*. New York: Cobblehill/Dutton, 1993.

Carlson, Judy. *Harriet Tubman: Call to Freedom*. New York: Ballantine Books, 1989.

Haskins, Jim. *Get on Board: The Story of the Undergound Railroad*. New York: Scholastic, 1993.

McGovern, Ann. *"Wanted Dead or Alive": The True Story of Harriet Tubman*. New York: Scholastic, 1965.

McMullan, Kate. *The Story of Harriet Tubman, Conductor of the Underground Railroad*. New York: Bantam Doubleday Dell, 1991.

Petry, Ann. *Harriet Tubman: Conductor on the Underground Railroad*. New York: Harper Trophy, 1983.

Sterling, Dorothy. *Freedom Train: The Story of Harriet Tubman*. New York: Scholastic, 1954.

Taylor, M. W. *Harriet Tubman: Antislavery Activist*. Philadelphia: Chelsea House, 1991.

FOR MORE INFORMATION

Harriet Tubman Organization
Makes available a brochure titled "African-American Heritage Tours, Dorchester County, Maryland"

424 Race Street
Cambridge, MD 21613
Phone: (410) 228-0401

National Park Service
Write and request a brochure titled "The Underground Railroad," which maps and describes railroad routes and briefly profiles most noted conductors.

U.S. Department of the Interior
1849 C Street, NW
Washington, D.C. 20240

Underground Railroad Initiative
Provides updated information on the National Park Service's study of the Underground Railroad, its routes and operations.

National Park Service
National Capital Field Area
1100 Ohio Drive, SW
Washington, D.C. 20242

Web site: www.nps.gov/undergroundrr

The Menare Foundation
Provides information on Underground Railroad routes, safe houses, conductors, and agents.

Web site: www.ugrr.org/ur-map.htm

Note: For a state-by-state (or province-by-province) listing of libraries, colleges, historical societies, and other institutions where primary sources can be found, visit this Web site: www.uidaho.edu/special-collections/east2.html

ACKNOWLEDGMENTS

Many people helped me by providing background information and photographs to be used in this book. Special thanks are due to Judith Bryant d'Oronzio for her interest in the project; Evelyn Townsend, Kay McElvey, and John Creighton, the Harriet Tubman Organization; Rochelle Bush, Harriet Tubman Center for Cultural Services; Mary Yearwood, and James Huffman, Schomburg Center for Research in Black Culture.

Special thanks are also due Cindy Silkworth, Rensselaer County Historical Society; Sal Alberti, James Lowe Autographs; Heather Egan, National Portrait Gallery; Malcolm Goodell, Cayuga County Historian; Samia Hakim, United South End Settlements, Harriet Tubman House; James T. Parker, Double Delta Industries; Stacy Elder and Susan J. LeClair, *U.S. News & World Report*; Alexandra Weinberg, Greater Philadelphia Tourism Marketing Corporation; Fern Cunningham, Frances C. Taylor, Don Wigal, and Tim Sullivan.

George Sullivan, New York City

PHOTO CREDITS

Library of Congress: 7, 14, 20, 23, 30, 36, 39, 63, 68, 74, 77, 89, 90, 93; George Sullivan: 12, 16, 28, 42; New York Public Library: 34, 47 (left), 48; Library Company of Philadelphia: 50; Scholastic Inc./Jim McMahon: 54; Deborah Bisson: 57; Author's Collection: 66; Alberti/Lowe Collection: 47 (right), 72, 107; Rensselaer County Historical Society: 83; Schomberg Center for Research in Black Culture: 95, 100, 110, 113; Cayuga County Historian: 103; Sophia Smith Collection/Smith College: 105; Champion Stamp Company: 115; U.S. New & World Report: 117.

INDEX

Bold numbers refer to photographs

ABOUT THE AUTHOR

George Sullivan is the author of a good-sized shelf of books for children and young adults. They cover a wide range of topics, from witchcraft to nuclear submarines; from baseball and field hockey to photography.

His interest in photography goes beyond just writing about it. He often takes photos to illustrate his books.

His other titles for Scholastic include Mr. *President: Facts and Fun About the Presidents, 100 Years in Photographs,* and *Alamo!*

For the In Their Own Words series, he has written biographies of Paul Revere, Lewis and Clark, Abraham Lincoln, and Helen Keller.

Mr. Sullivan was born in Lowell, Massachusetts, and brought up in Springfield, where he attended public school.

Mr. Sullivan graduated from Fordham University and worked in public relations in New York City before turning to writing on a full-time basis.

He lives in New York City with his wife. He is a member of PEN, the American Society of Journalists and Authors, and the Authors Guild.